# Table of Contents

1

# Introduction

Puppies. They're innocent, playful animals that lovingly curl up on our laps for warmth, but usually after they've left teeth marks on the wooden legs of the furniture located in the next room over, or have left an innocent trail of destroyed shoes around the house. As owners, we need to teach our dogs at a young age that their innocent, destructive habits and moments of disobedience aren't acceptable—"*no* bite," "*no* chew," "*no* eat," "*bad* boy." Instead, we need to shape our puppies and dogs into obedient, listening, rule-abiding members of our family and society—"sit," "stay," "lay down," "*good girl*."

They're very much like a human newborn in this sense. Both must be shaped into kind and gentle rule-abiding members of society. Toddlers and young children must learn early on that it's not okay to hit, talk back, and break rules. Likewise, puppies must learn early on that it's not okay to go to the bathroom in the house and disobey commands. Although the process of transforming children into law-abiding citizens is a lengthy process that continues, really, until they reach adulthood, shaping puppies into obedient members of society is a much shorter process. This is not to say, however, that it's always an *easier* process.

Whether you're a first-time dog owner or were raised surrounded my loyal family canines, training your dog can be quite the challenge. It's one thing to, as a child, see your parent train your dog. It's certainly another thing to *be* the one who must embrace the task. No matter your experience, you'll find incredibly helpful pieces of information and advice throughout this book that are guaranteed to make the dog training process go much smoother. You'll of course learn how to apply the most efficient training methods—clicker training or positive reinforcement—as you teach your puppy or dog the basic obedient and behavioral commands, but you'll also discover helpful suggestions about housebreaking your dog and eliminating the most common habits of destructive chewing, excited jumping, and excessive barking.

# Chapter 1—Before You Begin

Dog training is like teaching a child to write. It's a multi-step process that starts with small tasks, and then gradually increases to more complex tasks that require a particular set of When we're first taught how to write, we're not instructed on how to flawlessly craft cursive letters, nor are we expected to write long, complex paragraphs. We start by tracing dots that form each letter of the alphabet. Then, we practice writing each separate letter without the aid of dots. Then, we combine letters into small words, then bigger words, then sentences, and *then* paragraphs. It's a multi-step process that starts with small tasks, and then gradually increases to more complex tasks that require a particular set of foundational skills. Dog training is a very similar process. You can't simply bring your untrained puppy or dog home and expect him or her to sit, stay, fetch, dance, talk, and play dead on command. That would be like asking a 4 year old to write complete sentences in cursive. Instead, you start with the basics. You first teach your dog the basic command to "sit," just like a teacher would instruct a first grader how to write the letter "A." Make sense so far? Good, but there's a twist.

Actually, you'll need to do something *before* you even teach your new canine family member the basic commands. You'll of course need to buy the necessary supplies,—food, a food bowl, a collar, a leash, and perhaps a dog bed—but you'll also need to make a few pre-pooch decisions. Depending on your dog's age and training history, you'll need to determine what kind of training your dog needs. You'll also need to decide what kind of training method *you* want to use. If you're unfamiliar with current training categories and methods, you'll find this Chapter extremely helpful. I'll introduce and describe two of the four most common training categories. I'll also describe two of the most efficient and productive training methods you can adopt, along with each method's pros and cons. **Consistency** is a vital element during the training process, so it's ideal to have a training plan *before* you bring home your new family member.

## Training Categories

When we bring home our new puppy or dog, we usually have an idea of the commands and tricks we want to teach him or her. You might want to teach him the commands "sit" and "stay," someone else may want to teach him the commands "dance" and "play dead," while someone else may want to train him how to fetch. These are of course all *great* commands and tricks to teach your dog, but remember earlier when we said we need to start with the basics when training our dog? The same idea applies here. Training your dog to "fetch" won't go smoothly unless she's mastered the basic behavioral commands, just like training your dog to "play dead" won't go smoothly unless he's mastered the basic obedience commands.

Hopefully you're beginning to see the importance of determining what training category you'll begin your dog training with. Here's a list that describes each training category in a bit more detail and introduces what common commands fall under each. Keep in mind, though, that a few training methods—agility and vocational, for example—aren't listed here. These training methods come for more advanced puppies and dogs, but we're focusing on untrained puppies and dogs for this book.

**Obedience Training:** If you've just added an untrained puppy or dog to your family, this training category is a *must* and should be your *first* priority.

- **Commands:** "Sit," "Stay," "Come," and "Down" are the 4 most popular obedience commands *every* puppy or untrained dog should master.

- **Why?** Teaching your new puppy or dog these commands ensures you can control their actions. You'll be able to keep them safe, but you'll also make sure that they're welcome in front of others and are enjoyable to live with.

- **Behavioral Training:** Again, this training method is for untrained puppies or dogs. It should follow completion of obedience training, and it typically involves a combination of both commands and fun tricks.

  - **Commands:** "Speak," "Quiet," "Roll over," "Dance,"

"Play dead," etc.

- **Why?** Behavioral commands are used to shape, modify, and control your dog's behaviors. While some behavioral commands can be taught for pure entertainment value, others, such as "Quiet" are used to control your dog's instinctual desire to bark, therein ensuring that they make welcome house guests and polite citizens in public areas.

**Training Methods**

Although there are a multitude of training approaches circulating today, there are 2 methods that prove to work efficiently and successfully with dogs of all ages and breeds. What training method you chose to use with your dog is entirely your decision, of course,but there are a few factors you should consider as you decide. Here's a list that briefly describes each training method and lists the pros and cons of each:

- **Click Training:** This is by far the most popular dog training method, though it's also the newest technique. This training method, used by owners and certified trainers alike, uses a click sound to train a dog. When a dog completes a command, the owner or trainer clicks and rewards the dog with a treat. With practice, the dog associates the click sound with a treat, so that when you ask the dog to complete a command and it hears the click sound, it does so immediately knowing a reward is to follow.
  - **Pros:** Dogs are highly receptive to sounds, and this method takes advantage of their heightened awareness.
  - **Cons:** Because the dog has been trained to complete sounds after hearing a click, you'll always need to have a "clicking" device on you when making commands—one that makes the same or very similar noise.
- **Positive Reinforcement:** This is also a popular training method

that has been around for quite some time. It's also quite simple: You speak a command, and when the dog does it, you reward him or her with a food treat. They learn to associate a treat with following a command.

- ○ **Pros:** Dogs are quite receptive to the psychological concept of "association"—they associate following a command with food—so the results are quick and effective.

- ○ **Cons:** You'll typically always need to have a treat on you during the initial training period.

## Quick Things to Know

- Remember, each individual dog, not just breed, will vary, too. It's important to have a pre-pooch training plan, but you might need to readjust depending on your dog's individual personality.

- Dogs will be more receptive and less receptive to certain training categories, methods, and commands depending on their age. You'll find further information about this in Chapter 3.

- **Consistency** is a *must.* Switching training methods mid-way will only confuse your dog and possible erase the progress he or she has made.

- If you become annoyed, frustrated, or even angry while training your dog, stop what you're doing and refresh yourself. Dogs can actually *smell* fear and anger (from certain odors we emit when experiencing these emotions) and will become less receptive to your instructions and demands.

# Chapter 2—The 8 Basic Commands

Once you've settled which training category and method you're going to use with your new family member, and once you've brought home your new family member, of course, it's time to start training —sort of. Actually, you might want to hold off on any intensive for a few days after you've brought your puppy or dog home. This will be your dog's adjustment period. If he or she is a puppy, they'll need some time adjusting to being away from their mother and getting acclimated to their new environment. Matured dogs won't need as much time as puppies, but they'll certainly still require a few days to get used to their new environment.

However, this doesn't mean that your dog should be allowed to claim the cushiony living room carpet as their bathroom. Housebreaking—as we'll later see in the following Chapter—needs to start immediately. What we're talking about here, however, is teaching your dog the essential basic commands. In other words, you don't need to worry *too* much about teaching your puppy or dog how to sit, stay, and dance within the first week of them arriving. Play with them, care for them, and let them adjust before you get into the nitty-gritty details of training.

Once that grace period passes, however, it's time to get to work, starting with the basic obedience and behavioral commands. With that being said, this chapter will prove helpful for anyone looking for suggestions on how to train an untrained puppy or dog. I'll introduce the crucial obedience and behavioral commands that *every* trained dog should master, and I'll also provide some helpful advice for owners who are faced with training time restrictions.

### Basic Commands *Every* Dog Should Know

Dogs are highly malleable animals, which is why they have the ability to learn a wide range of commands and tricks within a reasonable short amount of time. This is especially nice if you've got a big family and everyone wants to teach your dog a wide assortment of tricks. While this is absolutely doable, especially among the smartest breeds of dogs—Poodles, German Shepherds, and Border Collies—you'll want to ensure that you teach your pooch a few *crucial* commands before getting into all those fun ones. I've included a list of 8 commands that *all* dogs should know, and what age puppies specifically should know each command by (assuming you bring your puppy home at 8 weeks old).

- **Sit.** (*9 weeks old*). No matter what age, dogs *will* get excited when it's time to go outside for a walk. Teaching the "sit" command will keep their excited jumping or pacing at bay while you put their leash on. It's also a great command to have on hand when out in public places. It's a way to control your dog, but it's also a way to prevent him or her from running off and getting hurt.

  **Training Myth #1:** A puppy has to be at least 6 months old to be properly trained.

  **Training Fact #1:** An awake puppy is a thinking puppy, and a thinking puppy is a trainable puppy.

- **Stay.** (*9 weeks old*). This command, again, is one used to tame an excited dog, keep them still, and ensure their safety.

- **Come.** (*10 weeks old*). This command is extremely useful when your dog is off the leash—whether roaming around the backyard or walking nearby. You'll be able to give your dog the freedom to roam, explore, and sniff around, but you'll also trust them to return to your side once you've told them to.

- **Drop it.** (*10 weeks old*) This is crucial to teach early on, especially for puppies that can and *will* turn *anything* you've left on the floor into their new favorite chew toy. If you can catch them early on, this command should hopefully save whatever chewy treasure your dog has found.

- **Off.** *(11 weeks old).*Whether big or small, dogs love jumping up on both familiar and unfamiliar people, but doing so can be more than just annoying. They all too often leave claw marks when they jump up, and heavier dogs oftentimes knock children over when they do so—albeit innocently. The "off" command is a quick and easy command to prevent an unwanted physical greeting.

- **Lay down.** *(11 weeks old).* If you have an easily excitable dog and frequent visitors at your house, "lay down" is a must. It helps your dog relax when surrounded by unfamiliar faces, sounds, and smells. It's also a great command to have handy if you live near the center of town and need to tie your dog up for a *brief* moment while you run into a store.

- **Quiet.** *(3 months old).* Most dog owners can't stand the perpetual sound of their dog barking, whether high or low pitched. "Quiet" is ideal because it lets your dog get your attention, but prevents him or her from continuing on after your attention has been captured and the possible disturbance resolved.

- **Leave it.** *(3 months old).* Dogs have an impressively strong noise, which is why they're sometimes adamant about stopping and sniffing during walks. Unfortunately, we don't have *all* day to wait around for them, which is why "leave it" is so useful. You'll get your puppy or dog moving again without having to tug on the leash or wrestle them away from their current preoccupation.

## Commands on a Time Restriction

The best time to welcome an untrained puppy or dog into your home is in the beginning of spring when the snow has cleared and/or the ground is dry. However, we sometimes aren't able to pick the season we being home puppies, and we certainly aren't able to take off work for weeks at a time to train our new family members. Actually, this is a pretty common occurrence. In fact, many dogowners find that their training sessions are in fact rushed. Fortunately, there are ways to train your dog on a deadline while still ensuring they're properly trained and equally obedient. Here are some helpful suggestions in case you or your family find yourselves in a similar situation:

- **Start with the "sit" command.** It's best if you can find the time to teach your dog "sit," "lay down," and "off," but if you're on a deadline, the basic "sit" command will do just fine. Here's why: we command our pets to "lay down" when they're pacing excitedly or nervously, and we command them to get "off" when they jump up on people or objects. A sitting dog can't do either of these actions, however, so the "sit" command has the ability to remedy not one but *three* obedience and behavioral issues or habits.

- **Identify your dog's *worst* habit and teach them the command that targets that one *first*.** It might be tempting to first teach your puppy or dog to "dance," "speak," or "play dead," but this won't do much in terms of shaping them into obedient family members. Once your dog has mastered "sit," identify their biggest weakness or bad habit—jumping up on furniture, barking at the rustling of leaves, chasing the cat incessantly around the house—and begin with that. Start with the habits that require the most attention and fixing, then work your way toward the minor ones using the limited time you have.

- **Teach one command at a time.** Having a time limit will probably tempt you into teaching your dog multiple commands at once in order to save time. In all actuality, it'll probably slow the process down. Dogs can of course multitask—to a certain degree—but puppies with high energy and a short attention span won't be able to focus for more than a minute or two on learning *one* command, let alone *three*. Let you puppy or dog learn, practice, and master one trick at a time, then move on to the next. It might seem like a slower process in the beginning, but it'll benefit both you and your dog in the long run.

## Quick Things to Know

- **You need to *show* your dog what you want.** Your puppy or dog needs to know and understand how to perform the desirable behavior before you can expect them to associate it with a verbal command or a visual signal. Take "dance" for example. You'll need to lift your dog's two front paws off the floor and hold him in a somewhat vertical position before you can expect him to do this by himself when you verbally say "dance."

- **Train your dog in different environments.** Sure, your dog might always respond to "come" when you say it in your house, but you can't expect him to automatically obey outside when he's surrounded by leaves blowing in the wind, the constant sound of birds, and the exciting scene of squirrels running up and down trees. However, training your dog to "come" both inside *and* outside will teach him how to ignore these fascinating objects when it comes time to.

# Chapter 3—Training at Different Ages

Although many of us think of our dogs as family members, best friends, or faithful companions, we view them as creatures entirely different from ourselves. Sure, they walk on 4 legs and have quite a different interpretation of what fun is, but they're also very much like us in some ways. Learning, surprisingly, happens to be one of these ways. Think about it. Many children and young adults these days have grown up with a tablet in their hand. They understood how to use a tablet at a very early age, so now all technological advances are easy things to master. They're very much like a puppy being trained in this way—impressionable and highly receptive. But does this mean that someone who *didn't* grow up using a tablet can't use or master it? Of course not. With practice and varying degrees of patience, anyone of any age can learn to use a tablet, and better yet, accomplish complex tasks using one. The same idea applies to older dogs. Just because they're older doesn't mean they can't learn new tricks. It just means they *might* need a little more practice time and you might need to be a *little* more patient while teaching them.

All this is to say, no matter your puppy or dog's age, he or she *can* be properly trained and taught new commands and tricks. Certain restrictions and challenges can of course pop up depending on your dog's physicality and mental state, but many of these factors, too, can be overcome. And of course there *are* ideal times to train a dog. A general rule of thumb is the younger, the better, but this absolutely doesn't mean you can't train your 10 year old German shepherd how to "speak," or your 12 year old Poodle how to "stay."

To help clarify some of these training-age misconceptions, I've included this helpful chapter that discusses age-specific techniques and restrictions of dog training. We'll take a specific look at training puppies and young dogs (6 weeks to 2 years old) and training older dogs (8 years to 12 years old).

## Training Puppies and Young Dogs

For puppies, the training rule of thumb is this: if your puppy awake, he or she can be trained. Unfortunately, many unknowing or inexperienced dog owners aren't aware of this, which means some puppies go months before receiving proper training. Furthermore, there's a common misconception that suggests puppies don't retain the information they're provided or the knowledge they learn until 3 or 4 months old. However, this just isn't the case. Dog breeder after dog breeder have vouched that this is a mere myth—hundreds have spoken out about their experiences and success with training 4-5 week old puppies how to sit, stay, and come.

So if you find yourself welcoming a young, energetic, 4-legged family member into your family, take some time to read the following information about age-specific training for puppies and young dogs (again, ages 6 weeks to 2 years old).

### Training deadlines

Although puppies and dogs can learn new commands and tricks at *any age*, beginning training *as soon as you bring home your puppy is ideal*. Most experts suggest:

- Your puppy should be fully trained before **6 months old**
- Waiting until after your puppy is 6 months old makes training a slower and more challenging process because they've developed bad habits that have gone unpunished and uncorrected

Think about it: a 6 month old puppy who has been allowed to run rampant around the house, chewing on whatever objects they can find within mouth's reach is going to be a lot harder to train than a 2 month old puppy who was taught immediately to leave objects alone when commanded. The 2 month old puppy has grown up knowing that this isn't okay; the 6 month old puppy will be utterly confused when you say his or her behaviors are no longer acceptable.

In Chapter 2 we provided a list of the 8 commands every puppy should know and at what age they should have mastered the commands by. You might find it helpful to review these commands and age deadlines if you've forgotten them.

## Training restrictions

*"Okay, my master has a treat and told me to sit, so now I'm going to—ball."*

Puppies are incredibly malleable creature when it comes to showing them what actions you like and what behaviors you dislike. However, many puppies are also:

- Highly energetic
- Have short attention spans
- Easily distracted
- Multi-minded

The simple jingle of keys in the next room over can quickly deter a puppy from their training and send them scrambling off to investigate the new and exciting sound. You'll need to be patient during this process. It's unavoidable —you can't glue your puppy's feet to the ground in order to ensure their undivided attention. Keep in mind that you *will* encounter challenges when training a puppy, but that the challenges you face in the first 6 months of training will be relatively simple and temporary compared to the ones you'll encounter should you wait to train until your pup is 6 months or older.

**Training Older Dogs**

Although some myths do circulate among training puppies, the myths that exist among training older dogs are far greater. And that's just it—they're myths. Dogs are smart creatures, no matter their age. Sure, training an older dog may require a different training deadline and may have different restrictions than a puppy, but it's still an entirely feasible task. Older dogs are very much like older people: a senior citizen can learn how to use the latest technological gadget with the right amount of instruction, practice, and patience, just like an older dog can learn how to "speak" with the right amount of positive reinforcement, practice, and patience from the their instructor.

## Training deadlines

Puppies have a suggested training deadline—ideally, a puppy will be completely trained by 6 months old. Mature dogs, on the other hand, don't fall within these perimeters. Training will really depend on each individual dog—their personal receptivity, their training history, their willingness to learn, and their intellect. You won't be able to set specific deadlines for when your dog will master a trick,—"Fluffy will learn to "dance" by next Tuesday," for example—but you can set deadlines that mark when you should stop your specific training if no results come forth—"If Fluffy doesn't master the "dance" command within the next 2 months, we'll move on." It'd be nice to advise you on a specific training deadline, but that's simply not possible with older dogs, unfortunately. Instead, you'll need to:

- **Gage:** Determine what your dog's physical and mental abilities are. *Will my dog's arthritis prevent her from going up on her back legs and learning the "dance" command?*

- **Judge:** Think about how the training is going so far. *Is my dog showing progress, or are our efforts unproductive?*

- **Adjust:** Reflect on your success and determine if there's something you can adjust in order to increase productivity. *What if I teach my dog to dance on all fours instead?*

- **Assess:** At the end of each week, assess your dog's progress. *My dog shows signs of progression. She's completed the command once or twice. I'll give it another month before reassessing again.*

### Training restrictions

The restrictions that tend to come with training older dogs are what probably fuels the saying, "you can't teach an old dog new tricks." But here's the thing: this saying includes *all* older dogs. However, there are plenty of older dogs that flawlessly learn new commands within days. For the dogs that struggle, it's not because they're not smart. It's because they have mental or physical restrictions that prevent them from following through with commands. Some of the most common reasons why older dogs face training restrictions are:

- **Arthritis:** Many older dogs will experience various forms of arthritis. Some dogs can carry on with daily physical activities without much effort, while others struggle to walk. Commands such as "dance," "roll over," "play dead," and "paw" might not be an option depending on your dog's arthritis location and progression, but commands like "stay," "lay down," "sit," "leave it," and "speak" might still be viable options.

- **Canine Cognitive Disorder:** This disorder, more commonly known as "Doggie Alzheimer's" alters your dog's mental state. Frequent disorientation, decreased hearing, restlessness, and decreased desires for physical activities can make it challenging to train your dog.

There are other restrictions that you'll want to consider when training your older dog. Keep in mind, however, that mental conditions, especially, aren't always physically seen. You may become frustrated after 3 months when your dog still hasn't learned to "speak," but his or her inability might stem from mental disorders. Because of this, we strongly recommend that you:

- **Talk to your vet before you begin training.** Your vet will be able to provide a full mental and physical work-up of your dog so that you know *beforehand* what commands or tricks won't be received or physically capable by your dog.

## Training Tips for Dogs of All Ages

Whatever your puppy or dog's age may be, it's crucial that you approach training with these ideas in mind:

- **Positivity.** Your puppy or dog needs to be a willing participant when it comes to learning new commands and tricks. Training isn't just about the owner—it's an interaction that requires motivation and willingness on *both* sides.

- **Patience.** A puppy is *going* to get distracted during training. There's no doubt about this. You'll need to be patient while you train them—learn what times of day they learn the best and take advantage of it. Likewise, an older dog *will* struggle to understand a new command when it's one that demands them to break a habit they've been allowed to do for years. Again, patience is crucial here—put yourself in your dog's shoes. Imagine what it would be like if someone told you to stop doing something you've been doing all your life.

# Chapter 4-Your Tone and Face

Although newborns are drastically less furry and aren't capable of leaving a path of destruction—torn shoes, half-eaten pencils, drool-ridden items from the trash—everywhere they go like puppies can, we tend to treat the two in very similar ways. We forgive a newborn's 2 a.m. crying just like we forgive a puppy's incessant 3 a.m. whimpering for his mother the first week he's away from her. We coo over sleeping newborns just like we coo over our puppies when they curl up and fall asleep in our laps. We even talk to newborns in the same sing-song, "baby-talk" tone that we all too often unconsciously adopt when we watch bright-eyed puppies innocently explore everything in their paths. But let's stop here because we've reached an important topic—our voice and face when we interact with dogs and puppies.

The way we state commands—in low or high-frequency tones—affects how our dog receives our commands, just like how our facial expressions—a welcoming smile or strict glare—affects our dog's receptivity and willingness to Your tone infliction and facial expressions play a major role during the training process. It seems like a nitty-picky or perhaps even irrelevant topic, but it certainly has more merit than many would believe. Actually, the way we state commands—whether in low or high-frequency tones—affects how dogs perceive us and receive our commands, just like how our facial expressions—a welcoming smile or a strict glare—affect our dog's receptivity and willingness to listen, learn, and obey.

Knowing the basics of both and how to use them to your advantage will help the training process go smoother.

**Your Training Tone**

As you think about the tone you're going to adopt while training your puppy or dog, it's important to keep a few, scientifically proven concepts in mind:

- **Dogs are highly responsive to "up-talking."** We've all done or heard "up-talking" before, you just might not have known that it actually had a name. Essentially, it's when our voice-pitch rises on the last word or words when asking a question. Imagine asking a dog "Do you want to go outside?" Did you notice what happened to your voice when you said "outside"? Dogs notice this, and you've probably noticed this, too, when your dog immediately picks his or her head up and stares at you waiting to hear more.

- **Dogs are more receptive to high-frequency sounds than low-frequency sounds.** Have you ever wondered why dog whistles are so effective at capturing a dog's attention? Well, this is why. A dog's hearing is quite extraordinary. It's far better than ours, especially when it comes to hearing high-frequency sounds. This is also why dogs respond better to our commands when we say things in higher pitched tones. It sounds lighter and happier of course, but it's also appealing to a dog's hearing strengths.

- **Strict isn't always best.** This idea stems from the idea above. That is, training and commanding your dog in a strict, low frequency voice isn't conducive to their learning or success. Their hearing isn't as sensitive when we speak in low tones, so their receptivity to our commands won't be as strong, either. But training dogs in a strict tone isn't helpful for general reasons, either. It'll make them feel uncomfortable, unnerved, or bad about themselves, therein limiting their receptivity.

## Your Training Face

Although our domesticated dogs are still, in many ways, very much like their wolf ancestors, they differ in one drastic way: wolves avoid eye contact at all costs while dogs are extremely receptive to our facial expressions and physical gestures. We've all encountered a dog whose gaze seems to reach our innermost selves. Well, there's actually some truth behind these feelings. Dogs read our facial expressions for information—*"where's the food?" "What have I done wrong?" "What are you thinking about me right now?"* Because our face serves as a source of information for our dogs, it's crucial that we have an awareness of our facial expressions during training. You'll want to keep these following ideas in mind:

- **Some training methods advise you not to blink. Don't do this.** A non-blinking face is one that oftentimes makes a dog feel wary or unsure of whether he or she is doing something wrong. Training your dog can already be a confusing time for him or her, so you'll want to avoid creating even more confusion with an unreadable training face.

- **The angry or annoyed glare will never do what you intend it to.** When our puppy or dog does something wrong, we of course want to let him or her know this, but you won't find success in condemning and correcting their behavior with an angry glare or annoyed stare. These facial expressions will only limit their receptivity to learning and willingness to practice. It's certainly hard *not to*, though, when they tear apart your favorite slippers or have emptied *all* the contents of the kitchen trash on the living room carpet. But when moments like these arise, show your puppy that he's done something wrong by saying "no" and pointing to the undesirable product of their behavior (the destroyed slipper or trash-filled living room) with a **neutral** facial expression.

# Chapter 5—Housebreaking

What's one thing every dog owner dreads? The unanimous answer is housebreaking their dog. It's probably one of the most challenging components to dog training, but it's also the most crucial. Training your puppy to use the bathroom *outside*—and not the comfy, padded living room carpet—is the *very first* thing you'll want to teach your puppy, even *before* you teach the basic command of "sit." But perhaps *before you even do that,* you'll want to familiarize yourself with the basics of housebreaking, if you're not already familiar with them.



Housebreaking your puppy or dog is crucial, so it's essential that you know the most accurate, efficient, and productive ways of doing so. This chapter will help you figure this out. We'll first outline a tested and proven bathroom schedule that you can follow with your puppy in the beginning days or perhaps weeks of training. Maintaining this schedule will be crucial. However, there's another equally important component to you and your puppy's success with housebreaking: your recognition of your pup's "bathroom signs." This chapter will walk you through the most common bathroom signs for puppies and dogs of all housebreaking stages so that you're able to understand and recognize your puppy's needs, no matter what point you two are at in the housebreaking process.

**Establishing a Schedule**

Here's the thing: you can have your puppy or dog fully housebroken in 7 days. With something as simple as a schedule, you'll drastically reduce accidents on the carpet and time spent on your hands and knees scrubbing out avoidable stains.

Puppies are very much like humans. They love schedules. They thrive off knowing when to expect something and when not to expect something. After all, your puppy quickly learns to expect a dish full of food when she hears the crinkling of the dog food bag and the sound of food hitting the bottom of the once empty bowl. Introducing a schedule into your dog's routine is very much like this—they'll know that as soon as they wake up that they get to go outside, that they go outside after they ate, and that they get to go outside again before bed.  Yet, owners *also* benefit from establishing a schedule. That is, we get to create a bathroom schedule that works best for *our own* daily routines. It's a win-win for both dog and owner, really. So, here's a great example of a schedule that will help progress your housebreaking training quickly along:

| Time: | Explanation: |
| --- | --- |
| **Early Morning** | You'll probably have to wake up a bit earlier than you're used to, but the key is this: get to your puppy before he or she wakes up, and bring them immediately outside. |
| **After Breakfast** | That is, immediately after breakfast. Digestion happens quickly with dogs, especially puppies, so let your dog eat, then direct them outside after they finish. |
| **During and After Playtime** | Playtime can last minutes or hours. You'll need to use your best judgement with this part, but it's best to take your dog outside every 30 minutes within the first 1-4 days, then every hour from the 5th-7th day. |
| **Before and After** | Playtime is always followed by naptime with puppies. When you sense your puppy getting tired, take them outside before they fall asleep. Likewise, |

| **Naptime** | take them outside as soon as they wake up from their nap. Unlike the morning schedule, you don't need to wake them up from their nap to take them outside. Just be sure you're around when they wake up—post-nap is the best time for accidents. |
| --- | --- |
| **During and After Playtime (again)** | The same instructions apply here as they did above. When you're able to gage your pup's bathroom signs, you'll no longer need to take them out every 30 minutes or every hour. |
| **After Dinner** | Again, take your puppy out immediately after he or she has finished eating dinner. |
| **Before Bedtime** | Take your puppy out right before bedtime, then let them sleep until you start the schedule again the next morning. |

**Recognizing the Bathroom Signs**

You'll notice that there's *a lot* of scheduled times when you should take your puppy outside to use the bathroom. It's certainly a lot, but it's worth it when you don't have to clean up accidents throughout the day. However, there's a helpful ways to loosen the regiment of the above schedule—identify and recognize your puppy's bathroom signs. Every puppy has them, no matter what stage they're at in the housebreaking process. You'll need to do some careful observing of your puppy to learn their individual signs, but you should find this list a helpful source in the meantime:

- **Untrained puppy bathroom signs.** Non-housebroken puppies are sneaky, clever creatures. Even at 8 weeks old they have some sense that what they're doing is unacceptable, and as a result, they hide. They sneak off to quiet places around the house when you're not looking—under the bed, in the closet, behind the couch, under the table. So, keep an eye on them. You'll want to watch out for:
    - **Sniffing** the floor, whether carpet, tile, stone, or hardwood
    - Venturing **behind furniture** or under tables

- ○ **Sniffing or pacing** around places they've had recent accidents

- **Semi-trained puppy bathroom signs.** A semi-trained puppy is beginning to understand that they need to go outside to use the bathroom, but they're usually still learning how to tell you this. Although they're typically not as sneaky as an untrained puppy, you'll still need to be aware of where they are. You'll also want to look out for a puppy that:

  - ○ **Glances** in your direction

  - ○ **Sits or lays near you** but doesn't get too comfortable

  - ○ **Whines, whimpers, or barks** in an attempt to get your attention

- **Trained puppy bathroom signs.** Trained puppies have had some time to develop more mature ways of getting your attention and telling you that they need to go outside. What's great about this is that you generally don't even need to train them to go near the door when they need to use the bathroom. They instinctually associate the door with using the bathroom (if you've been taking them outside using the same door, that is.) A trained puppy will:

- **Stand, sit, or lay down** by the door.

- Patiently **sit in front of you** or **next to you** and make frequent or constant eye contact.

- **Quickly bark** or make a noise.

## Your Training

It might sound a bit ridiculous, but you'll need to train yourself as well. No, you don't need to housebreak yourself, but you *do* need to train yourself in a few specific areas in order to ensure your dog finds housebreaking success and that you don't lose your mind during the (hopefully quick) process.

- **Understanding.** Dog owners, especially first time dog owners, have the tendency to get frustrated and angry with their puppy when they have accidents. Although your frustration may in fact be reasonable when your pup chooses to use your pillow case as a bathroom pad, you need to understand that they're not doing it maliciously. They simply *just don't get it, yet.* The best thing you can do in situations like this is to take a deep breathe, reprimand your puppy by saying "no" while pointing to the accident, take them outside for a few minutes, the clean up the mess. When you combine the schedule provided above with recognizing your puppy's bathroom signs, the frequent accident will turn into the occasional accident, the occasional accident will turn into the infrequent accident, and the infrequent accident will turn into the nonexistent accident. In other words, the accidents are only temporary.

- **Observe and recognize your puppy's bathroom signs.** I mentioned this above, and I'm reiterating it now because it's a crucial element in housebreaking your new family member. No matter their age, your dog *will* tell you when they need to go out, it's simply a matter of recognizing how they tell you. Although I listed the common bathroom signs for dogs at all housebroken stages, you might benefit further by knowing a few less common yet equally important bathroom signs your dog may use to get your attention:

    o Intentionally stepping in front of you or getting in your

way

- o Pawing or jumping up on you

- o nuzzling whatever body part they can reach

- o Sitting on top of you but constantly fidgeting

**Why all of this is important:** If you want to housebreak your puppy or dog quickly and efficiently, you'll need to meet him or her half way. They'll stop having accidents in the house and learn to use the bathroom outside *if* you pay attention to and act upon their bathroom signs immediately. But most importantly, **ignoring your puppy's cues that they have to go outside undercuts the progress you've made** because it shows them that *they don't control when they go outside, you do.*

# Chapter 6—Chewing, Jumping, and Barking

Although they're terribly cute creatures who easily melt our hearts, puppies are mercilessly destructive. They leave a wake of destruction wherever they go. Leave them alone for 5 minutes and you'll enter your bedroom to find 5 *left foot* (only) shoes strewn around the room, each with its own set of unique damage—your sneakers will inevitable be missing the souls, your work shoes will be lace-less, and your casual shoes will be sporting a fine layer of puppy drool. Divert your attention from the kitchen for more than 3 minutes and your puppy will have sniffed out the trash and somehow managed to carry trash particles piece-by-piece to the living room floor. Perhaps this is why puppies are genetically disposed to cuteness—to keep us from getting too angry when they destroy our valuable belongings or make messes throughout the house.

But here's the good news: your dog's undesirable can be erased or corrected without *too much* of an effort on your behalf. This is good because you'll be able to break your puppy's habits without needing to sacrifice the time you spend teaching them the obedience and behavioral commands we introduced earlier in Chapter 2. With that being said, this chapter will discuss the 3 most common bad puppy habits—chewing, jumping, and barking—and how to correct them.

## Chewing

Incessant chewing—on anything and everything, really—is one of the most common, if not consistent, bad habits puppies instinctually do. But that's just it—chewing is an instinct. Here's why:

### Why do dogs chew?

Puppies, and dogs for that matter, have incredibly sensitive noses. They have the unique ability to pick up on human smells, especially the ones we as humans are incapable of identifying. From across the house they can smell the wide variety of oils and sweats we emit, and they're able to recognize us by our own *personal* smells. So, then, why do puppies continually go after our slippers and shoes? Besides the fact that the material simply feels nice to chew on (especially with teething pups), objects that are in prolonged contact with the smell-heavy areas of our body,—shoes and slippers that we wear on our feet, for example—remind our dog of *us*. When we leave our puppy alone for periods of time, he or she wants to be with us, so they chew on the objects that best remind them of us.

### How do I solve it?

Fixing this habit is a rather simply procedure, thankfully. Here's what you need to do:

**1.** When you catch your puppy chewing on something they shouldn't be—a slipper, shoe, a book, the wooden leg of furniture—make a loud noise that distracts them from what they're doing.

**2.** Offer your puppy an acceptable toy instead, preferably one that has your scent on it. (You may want to have a few, new toys stashed away in your closet for these occasions, toys which you've wrapped in worn clothing articles so they smell like you).

**3.** Reward your puppy with a treat when they take the new toy you've offered in their mouth and forget about the object they were chewing on before.

## Jumping

Jumping—generally out of excitement when family members return home or new guests arrive—is one of the bad puppy habits that oftentimes go uncorrected. And if you have a large dog breed—anything that weights over 30 pounds, really—this bad habit quickly turns into an awful habit. You'll want to make eliminating this habit a priority if you entertain guests frequently—no one enjoys a jumping dog that leaves irritated scratch marks and nearly knocks them over.

### Why do dogs jump?

Dogs have a strange fascination with urine—we oftentimes think they use urine to mark territories, but recent studies suggest that this might actually be a dog's way of posting a bulletin about themselves to the dog public—their age, their neighborhood, their sexual maturity, and their compatibility with other dogs. With all of this comes sniffing—it's the way other dogs "read" these doggy bulletins. But how does all this relate to jumping, you ask? Well, think about it. We've all met a dog whose first action is to sniff us out—our hands, our feet, our legs, and our groin. They're trying to "read" us by sniffing out urine. Smaller dogs are of course lower to the ground, which is why jumping is especially common among smaller breeds. They need to jump in order to sniff us out in the places they want.

### How do I solve it?

Fortunately, there's a pretty simple way to quickly put an end to your puppy or dog's jumping habit:

**1.** When you enter the house, immediately offer your hand. Your hand will be riddled with plenty of interesting scents for your dog to gather information from—where you've been, what you were doing, who you were with. This should deter them from needing to sniff out further information, and therefore, from jumping.

**2.** If this simple remedy doesn't work, teach your dog the "lie down" command.

**3.** With a treat in hand, ask your dog to "sit." When they do this, let him or her sniff the treat.

**4.** Slowly lower the treat to the floor, making sure your dog's eyes and nose follow. When they've lowered their nose, let them briefly lick or sniff the treat.

**5.** Do this until your dog's elbows touch the floor. You may need to apply some pressure to the middle of their back to show them that you want them to lie down. Reward them with the treat when they *fully* lie down.

**6.** Add the command "lie down" as your dog completes the action.

**7.** Practice. In time, your dog will have mastered the "lie down" command which means you'll be able to prevent them from jumping up when you or guests enter the house.

## Barking

Although specific dog breeds are more prone to barking than others, all dogs do it. Barks come in low, guttural rumbles, in high-pitched yips, and everything in between. The thing is: most dog owners find these natural noises to be quite annoying, especially when there's really no need for them —the faint howling of the wind outside or the sound of the neighbor's children playing across the street can set our dogs off.

### Why do dogs bark and make noises?

Much like how humans communicate by making guttural sounds within our mouths, dogs communicate by barking. However, recent studies have shown that the different sounds our dogs make indicate different messages. For example, high-frequency barks—whines, whimpers, and squeals—indicate pain or a craving for attention. Moans and grunts, surprisingly, indicate contentment. Growls and snarls are of course sounds of aggression or signs of potential danger. A howl represents a search for communication with other nearby dogs. But perhaps most interestingly, the sound of a panting dog seems to indicate laughter or excitement. As you can see, there's a wide range of noises that convey a wide range of messages. The rule of thumb for barking, however, is this: lower barks convey danger and higher barks convey companionship.

**How do I solve it?**

So you've got a noisy dog who seems to bark at inappropriate times. Here's how to remedy the bad habit:

**1.** *Before taking any action,* take a day or two to keep track of when your dog barks and what context it happens in. Does it happen when visitors arrive at the door? Does your dog whimper as you read or do something? The former context indicates you'll want to control your dog's barking, but the latter context suggests your dog might need something else—attention perhaps.

**2.** Decide at what times you want your dog to bark—perhaps when someone arrives at the door—and at what times you deem their barking inappropriate —perhaps when they see the cat outside the window.

**3.** Teach your dog the "quiet" command.

**4.** Grab a handful of treats every time you hear your dog barking. Stand in front of them and command "quiet" as they bark.

**5.** When they stop barking and you have their complete attention, praise them and reward them with a treat.

**6.** Do this every time your dog barks inappropriately. Eventually, your dog will learn the "quiet" command so that you can immediately stop their barking during the times you wish. With enough practice and perhaps a little bit of luck, your dog might even learn to avoid barking during certain situations altogether.